Roads - The birds

se

hrew his Hat away -

lung - The Breezes broug

ed them in the Glee -

ngle Flag, And signed th

r went out at Noon -

Farm - Then stepped

rmament And rested

together bore away Upo

To the mystery that is Emily —J. B.

For Mom and Dad —B. S.

Emily Dickinson Daguerreotype courtesy of the
Amherst College Archives & Special Collections.

Library of Congress Cataloging-in-Publication Data:

Names: Berne, Jennifer, author. | Stadtlander, Becca illustrator.
Title: On wings of words : the extraordinary life of Emily Dickinson / by
Jennifer Berne ; illustrated by Becca Stadtlander.
Description: San Francisco : Chronicle Books, 2020.
Identifiers: LCCN 2017033710 | ISBN 9781452142975 (alk. paper)
Subjects: LCSH: Dickinson, Emily, 1830-1886—Juvenile literature. | Poets,
American—19th century—Biography—Juvenile literature.
Classification: LCC PS1541.Z5 B445 2017 | DDC 811/.4 [B]—dc23 LC record available
at https://lccn.loc.gov/2017033710

Manufactured in China.

Design by Amelia Mack and Jill Turney.
Typeset in Walker and Becca Wings.
The illustrations in this book were
rendered in gouache and watercolor.

10 9 8 7 6 5 4 3 2 1

Chronicle Books LLC
680 Second Street, San Francisco, California 94107

Chronicle Books—we see things differently.
Become part of our community at www.chroniclekids.com.

On Wings of Words

THE EXTRAORDINARY LIFE OF EMILY DICKINSON

BY JENNIFER BERNE   ILLUSTRATED BY BECCA STADTLANDER

chronicle books·san francisco

Soft moonlit snow draped the Dickinson house in white.

It reaches to the Fence—
It wraps it, Rail by Rail,
Till it is lost in Fleeces—
It flings a Crystal Veil

In a little room—in the dark before dawn—

a baby girl was born.

Her parents celebrated the holiday

they called Emily.

Emily met the world. And began to explore.

To little Emily, every bird, every flower, every bee
or breeze or slant of light seemed to speak to her.

She explored with her eyes, her ears, her thoughts—

and found new words for
everything she was discovering.

The bee is not afraid of me,
I know the butterfly . . .
The brooks laugh louder
when I come.

When thunder crashed
and lightning flashed,
Emily got scared and called it . . .

the fire.

Emily adored her older brother, Austin.
She said, "there was always such
a Hurrah" wherever he was.

She loved her school friends, who she said were . . .

A warmth as near as if the Sun
Were shining in your Hand.

Every day Emily's life rippled with new joys,
And swayed with new feelings.

It was clear Emily was becoming a person—
in many ways like other people—only more so.

Her happys were happier. Her sads were sadder.

Her thoughts were deeper. Her desires were stronger.

And oh, there was so much that Emily loved.

My heart grows light so fast that I could
mount a grasshopper and gallop around the
world, and not fatigue him any!

Most of all, Emily loved her books.

The strongest friends
of the soul— BOOKS.

To Emily every book was an adventure, a distant journey on a sea of words. And if a book was forbidden, well, that didn't stop Emily . . .

Like the book she wanted, that Austin smuggled into the house and hid inside the piano. Emily rushed it up to her room and read it in delicious secrecy.

Every story she read at night by candlelight, or in the garden's midday sun, was a new passion—a ray of light.

But there were shadows, too.
In the 1800s, sorrow was a
daily companion.
The sorrow of
diseases incurable,
accidents untreatable.
And deaths too soon,
too close.

All this frightened Emily.
And flooded her mind
with questions.

Emily tried to
find answers
at home.

She looked
for answers at
her church.

She searched for
answers at school.

But everywhere she looked,
she was told to obey without asking,
to believe without knowing why.

So she began to put her faith in
what she could see and understand.

In the name of the Bee—
And of the Butterfly—
And of the Breeze—Amen!

When her very religious school principal
separated the class into "Hopers" and "No-Hopers,"
Emily was put in the group without hope.
Yet Emily did have hope. Her own kind:

"Hope" is the thing with feathers—
That perches in the soul—
And sings the tune without the words—
And never stops—at all—

So—with her hope—
she sought her truth.

I am out with lanterns,
looking for myself.

Then—like rays of sun breaking
through the clouds—

her thoughts and feelings
started to come to her as words.

New words.

Her own words.

The robins, bumblebees, and daisies she loved—the dark diseases and frightening deaths—the unknowable God and mysterious heaven—all came pouring out, as poems.

Things are budding, and springing, and singing.

Answers she couldn't find in other people, she started to find in herself.

I have been dreaming, dreaming a golden dream, with eyes all the while wide open.

Her poems soothed her sadness.

Gave her strength. Set her free.

With the power of her words—

and the freedom of her imagination—

she tasted spices in foreign lands,

and hid inside a flower.

She leaned against the sun,

dwelt in a house of possibilities,

and rode a carriage to the ends of time.

She became a bird, a worm, a ghost, a god.
A beggar, a king, a somebody, a nobody.

I'm Nobody!
Who are you?
Are you—Nobody—too?
Then there's a pair of us!
Don't tell! They'd banish us—you know!

How dreary—to be—Somebody!
How public—like a Frog—
To tell your name—the livelong June—
To an admiring Bog!—

She called her poems

my letter to the World That never wrote to Me

And so, with her words, her mind—
Emily dove into the darkest depths of
the sea, and of sadness. She rose up to the
glowing heights of the sun, and of joy.

Emily saw the inner world was
bigger than all the world outside.

The Brain—is wider than the Sky—
For—put them side by side—
The one the other will contain
With ease—and You—beside—

Emily spent more and more time in her room.
Writing, creating. She ventured out less and less.
Exhilaration—is within—

As Emily's inner world grew bigger, her outer
world grew smaller. Yes, there were things she
still loved in the worldly world.

She loved her gardens. The bees, the springtime,
and the wind combing its fingers through the
trees. And of course her family, a few very
special friends, her big dog, Carlo—and children—
Emily always loved children.

But most people, she saw rarely, or not at all.

Emily began to dress in white. White like clouds.
Like the foam on a wave.

White, like a cocoon in her room from which
butterflies were born. Butterflies that were
poems that flew—with Emily—on wings of words.

People in the town said Emily was weird, Emily
was strange. But Emily didn't care what they said
of her. Her world was somewhere else.

My Country is Truth.

Emily never stopped writing—
never stopped exploring.

With every day and every poem—she saw
more, discovered more, traveled deeper,
soared higher. For the rest of her life.

On a Saturday in May, 1886—Emily died—
slipping into the eternity she had wondered
about and written about all her life.

Then something wonderful and amazing happened.

Emily's sister, Vinnie, opened drawers, trunks, boxes, and closets—and found hundreds and hundreds of Emily's poems. More than anyone ever imagined. Poems that—on the wings of Emily's words—flew out and away—into the future and around the world.

Today almost every library, every bookstore,
every school in every city, state, and country
has Emily's poems. Emily's words, Emily's letters to
each of us.

*The world is sleeping . . . we must
be crowing cocks, and singing larks,
and a rising sun to awake her.*

And, in those words, can you hear Emily's voice
echoing through the years—speaking to you—to
all of us who are brave enough to take pen in
hand—to look deep—and write what we discover?

I dwell in Possibility—
A fairer House than Prose—
More numerous of Windows—
Superior—for Doors . . .

Of Visitors—the fairest—
For Occupation—This—
The spreading wide my
narrow Hands
To gather Paradise—

ABOUT EMILY'S POETRY

Many of Emily's poems are like puzzles or little mysteries—full of hints and riddles, visions, secrets, and truths—waiting to be discovered and experienced. Each one is inviting you to enter it and go on a thought journey with Emily.

No one fully understands or gets everything out of Emily's poems on the first reading. Often, if you reread a poem of Emily's a month later, a year later, many years later, you will see and find whole new things—new messages, new ideas, new currents—that never seemed to be there before.

As you evolve, so do Emily's poems. That's how full and rich they are. And that's why so many people fall in love with Emily's poems for their entire lives. I am one of those people. Perhaps you will be, too.

DISCOVERING THE WORLD OF POETRY

Reading

I think it's a good idea to start reading poetry just as Emily did—by reading many different poets. There are some wonderful books of collected poetry for young readers—books with wide varieties of poets and poetry, including some of the same poets Emily read and loved when she was a child.

You don't know which poet will open the door to poetry for you and invite you in. But that's part of the adventure—the exciting road that lies before you—in the land that is poetry.

Writing

One of the best ways to become a poetry reader is to also become a poetry writer. Read a little, write a little. Don't worry—no one's writing is great at the start. But if you're willing to bumble around a little and experiment, you'll be amazed how far it can take you and how much fun it can be.

The way to do it is just like walking. Take one step at a time, and before you know it, you're getting somewhere.

Sharing

One of the joys of reading poems is talking about them with other people—talking about the ideas in them, the hidden messages, the themes, the images, the stories running through them, and what they mean especially to you. How are they like your life and your experiences?

Sharing the poems you read and the poems you write, opens doors, expands your world, and deepens your friendships in ways nothing else possibly could.

Books by and about Emily

Emily's words:

Johnson, Thomas H., ed. *The Complete Poems of Emily Dickinson.* New York: Back Bay Books, 1976.

Johnson, Thomas H., ed. *The Letters of Emily Dickinson.* 3 vols. Cambridge, MA: Belknap Press, 1976.

About Emily:

Habegger, Alfred. *My Wars Are Laid Away in Books.* New York: Modern Library, 2002.

Sewall, Richard B. *The Life of Emily Dickinson.* Cambridge, MA: Harvard University Press, 2000.

AUTHOR'S NOTE

Every writer, every poet, every reader will probably have their own definition of poetry. Here is mine. Poetry is a deep exploration of each subject the poet approaches. An exploration that starts with the poet looking, feeling, thinking. Wondering. Imagining. Discovering.

Then—and this is the magic of poetry—through that exploration, words begin to emerge. Words flow into the writer's mind. Words that become phrases, sentences, ideas. New ones, that no one has ever thought or said before.

Now the writer begins to play with those words—arranging, rearranging, adding, subtracting, building, sculpting, until everything feels just right—until their creation feels complete. That is the birth of a poem.

That, to me, is poetry.

I'll let Emily end this book. Here are two stanzas, from one of my favorite poems of hers, in which she tells us how important she felt it was to be a poet.

I reckon—when I count at all—
First—Poets—Then the Sun—
Then Summer—Then the Heaven of God—
And then—the List is done—

But, looking back—the First so seems
To Comprehend the Whole—
The Others look a needless Show—
So I write—Poets—All—

ARTIST'S NOTE

The illustrations in this book come from actual historical images whenever possible, maintaining historical accuracy while also allowing the imagery of the story to shine. The house depicted in this book, for example, is the house Emily Dickinson was born in and the one she lived in for most of her life. To avoid confusion, I have rendered it as it was at her death and as it stands now, a National Historic Monument and Museum to Emily Dickinson.

However, the real joy of illustrating this book was in the more abstract ideas of Emily's writing. To interpret this poetry visually was a challenge that broke through my usual way of thinking and helped me grow as an artist. I love painting butterflies and saw them as a theme throughout the book, representing Emily's relationship to nature and the beauty of her work. My hope is that young readers will see the things they love in these images and be inspired by Emily's words.

Pearls - What Neckla

replaced, in Hoisted

sung - The Sunshine

The Bushes - spangles

dejected Lutes - And ba

The Orient showed a s

fête away. Two Butterfli

And waltzed above a

straight through the